THE FOUR RINGS

New and Selected Poems

THE FOUR RINGS

New and Selected Poems

FRED DINGS

STEPHEN F. AUSTIN STATE UNIVERSITY PRESS

For information about permission to reproduce selections from this book, contact *permissions* :

Stephen F. Austin State University Press
P.O. Box 13007, SFA Station
Nacogdoches, TX 75962
sfapress@sfasu.edu
www.sfasu.edu/sfapress
936-468-1078

Project Manager: Kimberly Verhines
Cover Art: Barbra Riley "Downfall at Nightfall"

ISBN: 978-1-62288-304-2
First Edition

Acknowledgments and Credits

Bloomsbury Review	"Paper Bridge"
Carolina Quarterly	"Swallows at a Quarry Lake"
Chicago Quarterly Review	"After Picking up My Son from Kindergarten"
Context South	"The Concession"
Denver Quarterly	"After the Solstice"
High Plains Literary Review	"Dissertation on Dogs" "Planes" "Transitory Music"
Ironwood	"Padre Island"
James Dickey Newsletter	"The Image"
The New Republic	"Redwing Blackbirds" "Sycamores" "Riva Looking Towards Sirmione" "Matthew 6: 9-13"
The New Yorker	"Late Marsh"
Miramar	"La Farge: Entrance to the Tautira River, Tahiti, *Fisherman Spearing a Fish*"
The Packinghouse Review	"Words for My Wife" "The Fish" "The Gentle Fire"
Paris Review	"Dido" "The Migrant Couple" "Sunday Evening" (as "The Evening After")

Poet Lore	"In the Season of Memory"
Poetry	"Chains of Change"
	"The Fire"
	"Letter to Genetically Engineered Superhumans"
	"The Man and the Cemetery Effigy"
	"Migratory Flight"
	"The Past"
	"Revelations"
	"Words for a Perfect Evening"
Quarterly West	"Japanese Screen"
Salt	"The Moment"
Shenandoah	"Crabbing"
South Florida Poetry Review	"One Reason for This"
Spillway	"A Genetically Engineered Superhuman Laments"
TriQuarterly	"The Bodily Beautiful"
	"The Case Against Daedalus"
	"Claims of the Past"
	"Eulogy for a Private Man"
	"The Unlived"
	"Woman with Gravitas"
U.S. Catholic	"Spheres"
Wallace Stevens Journal	"The Bridge"
	"Children and Death"
Western Humanities Review	"The Glowing Coal"
	"The Last Voyage"

World Literature Today   <u>Print</u>:
"Meditation Caves of Tibet"
<u>Online</u>:
"Independence Day"
"The Blue Whale"
"Making Soap Bubbles with My Daughter"
"Late Autumn"
"Stage IV"
"Stopping at a T-Intersection in Late Autumn"

"That Day." In *One for the Money: The Sentence as a Poetic Form.* Lynx House Press.

"The Divers." In *Literature: Reading and Writing with Critical Strategies* by Steven Lynn. New York: Longman.

For Maria, Madison, and James

The secret
Of this journey is to let the wind
Blow its dust all over your body,
To let it go on blowing, to step lightly, lightly
All the way through your ruins...

— James Wright, "The Journey"

Contents

The Four Rings: New Poems

FROM *After the Solstice*

Redwing Blackbirds

This morning they came like the dying
reclaiming their old lives, delirious
with joy right on the seam of Spring,
streaming in by the tattered thousands
like black leaves blowing back onto the trees.

But the homeless know what's expected by now,
and when the farmer fired into their body,
they rose all around me like trembling
black wounds gaping red at the shoulders,
a river of pain draining into the sky.

Tonight, as I look at the cold sky
and its flock of blue-white scars,
I can't yet turn from Orion's red star,
whose trembling red light has travelled for years
to die now into any eyes that will hold it.

Sycamores

As a child I was enchanted by their white branches,
their cool lightning veining dark woods along streams,
but soon was disappointed they were not pure white
and here and there were blotched gray-green.
I see them in a different light now, here in Assisi,

the sun splashing everywhere, swallows sickling the air,
as a girl unshutters her window and waters the geraniums
you see flaming the sills eternally in Italy.
While one arm pours and the other tends the soil,
her skin is clearly unmarred as it brindles

with the olive shadows of the rich green leaves.
Perhaps the blotches of death we so fear when they appear
in the light of age are really the harmless shadows
of something our whole lives have been carefully tending,
something unseen perhaps, but vitally green.

Riva Looking Towards Sirmione

for James Wright

At the stem end of the great blue pear of Lake Garda
between Alps where the rain has just slashed,
a rainbow arcs among the clouds' blue rocks.
Lake water trembles between stone shoulders,
the same color as the storm-ashened sky.
Haze hovers there like a white fence
between the heavy gun-metal blue water
and the sculpted blue vapors in high winds.
The algae on the boat dock steps underwater
are no less green than the trees on the mountains.
Rain pocks the body of the lake into thin skins of water
which reflect for a moment, then are gone.

SWALLOWS AT A QUARRY LAKE

Though it might have been better never
to have dipped so deeply for our needs,
the earth is answering with the patience of water
as from a stone ledge on a cliff's face
a mother swallow teaches her child
how to feed on insects from the water's surface
while each time the young one dives too harshly
and splashes down, destroying the water's clear vision.
So he is called back to the stone
ledge to watch as she falls freely,
then banks and turns and follows
the elegant scythe of her wings
to just bring her mouth to its need,
stitching lightly across the surface,
leaving delicate rings widening and wedding
on the fragile threshold of the air.

Diptych

I. A Last Request

When night comes with his censer, strewing smoke,
and the road darkens, the road I love most because it leads
nowhere, I want enough time to remember a few small kindnesses
given freely and the way you looked one summer evening long ago,
I want enough time to touch the whole rosary of moments
I have lived by, so that, when my life exhales from my body,
it may be with a fullness that is whispered
like a carefully gathered prayer into the ear of time.

II. Matthew 6: 9-13

Blue herons that fish in silence, webs that sag with dew,
old pines in mist, the snow at sea,
and hues as they merge in evening,
rain on mossed rocks, and crackling flames,
and a breeze touched with brine,
and leaf-stained light in autumn, Gandhi, Bach, Monet, Maria,
and a stream pool laved with pollen, the surf as it lathers
and then hisses on the beaches,
the twilight, the stillness
: these things

The Pine Ridge

Tripping on rocks she went up the draw
to that razorback ridge where the topmost pines
bristle and fray against the sky.
She went among that stand of Ponderosas
which in time have claimed the entire hillside
with their scaly bark as dry as cracking flesh
and needles like thirst-clenched leaves.
And on the many layered net of fallen
needles (through which nothing grows)
you'll find discharged cones flared and still
spined though there are no seeds to guard
and perhaps a young doe lying with some comfort
the way a mind might couch
even on painful memories, dried and fallen into patterns,
if it does not turn too roughly upon them.
She stayed there for hours until the sun lowered
away and the pine ridge, as if tired of bright heat,
slowly turned its back—about the time
trees seem to soften and grow fragrant
and the lengthening shadows ease this way like a slow blue river
or the long blending fingers of an uncertain hand.
She came with her head slightly lowered and turned
as if listening to something I could not hear.

The Concession

Circuit-worn and tired, in a snow-filled forest,
I came to a small clearing
where a trapped beaver humped down against the snow
like a beaten child or dog cowed by his barking master.
I don't know why it came outside
its warm ice-glazed lodge of logs and branches
where one cool glide retrieved all needs
from a cache of tender twigs,
but when I saw his frightened cloudy eyes,
I shuffled slowly closer on my knees
as carefully as one approaches a memory of great injury
and spoke in an assuaging monotone
as gently as a mother might caress.
Its right leg stretched taut as rope
fraying to bone; its whole being strained
opposite forged rings staked at the center
in a circle of worn snow. It seemed
like a darkened moon in endless apogee
or the clubfooted hand of a clock's face
forever measuring the radius and cycle of its time.
I had hoped, with one quick sleight of hand,
to snap open the steel jaw
and unsnag its whole body.
When I reached, its censoring teeth
snapped at my fingers
and would have cut had I been slower.
I raised my foot to crush its skull,
but then thought better
and left the animal to gnaw itself off,
fall pelt or prey,
or freeze in its frozen zero.

ONE REASON FOR THIS

Mrs. Cavagna's farm is a brief staircase of terraces
above the valley where the Ticino River, straitjacketed
in concrete, spears straight into Lago di Maggiore.
The few grapevines are trained in rows of wishbones
along wooden trellises and each year raise themselves
on tendrils of child-wood curling question marks
over the dead. A black serpentine of asphalt flows
through her land like a river of grief down to Locarno
and ribbons up along the razoring mountainside to Monti Motti
from where I had just come from drinking cappuccino
and stopping to examine in a stone wall on the inside
elbow of a hairpin an empty sleeve of skin
a snake had lodged deliberately in tortuous meanders
among the rocks to push from the center of the old.

A storm was laboring against the mountain,
its breath getting colder and faster, its swollen
blue body threatening to unseam, and she
was hurrying to save from rain-rot the hay
that her wintering goats would transform into milk.
She was glad to see me, her new neighbor,
and smiled with a winter face that has seen the wind
and carries its bootprint as do snowdrifts and dunes
and welcomed me with her hands so hardened in layers
from years of guiding the scythe's moon-sliver of steel
past her feet that even if one of the butterflies
winking from the unmown tatters at the field's edge
would have at last come and landed in her palm,
she would have seen it, but not felt it.
As I worked to help her, her vertebrae screamed
to unpile until she locked in a grimace
and was forced to the house, the unpaned windows
flaming with geraniums, the stones straining at the mortar

like lost children the mountain was calling back home.
So I stood alone on that Ticino mountainside,
wrapped in wind beneath a lowering blue palm,
raking the earth-hair in mounds the wind
wanted to unpile, as did generations before me,
the hard whip of necessity cracking the cadence
of their lives. And I thought how so many now,
less bound but not more free, tired and afraid,
duplicate their days in a long diminuendo of the past
they call the present, sleepwalking through the miracle
of slow death, settling like a stylus in the most indirect
spiral inward they can find, breaking off and repeating
at the grooveless land around the totem of the world.

I let the rake-teeth settle among the stubble,
caressing the unexplored center beneath my feet,
wondering how long Mrs. Cavagna could go on
like the farm's one leg since her husband died,
each autumn staining her bare feet into burgundy boots,
marching the blood out of the grapes into the bottles
laid in the stonewalled cellar in rows like emerald
ships sailing into time until the day the blood becomes wine,
becomes spirit, and flows through the mouth into clearer glass,
into another mouth, another body, down
through the layers of pain to places still so tender
even the gentle fingers of the soft Merlot bring tears
streaming like run-off from the thawing soul.
That is how I found her with her bare table
and empty glass when I came like a clubfoot
eclipsing her doorway in from the rain,
not close enough to come any closer
as she strained to hide her embarrassment.
So not knowing what to do, I said
goodbye as kindly as I could and walked out,
drenching in the run-off from the sky.

After the Solstice

I was in the albergo on Via Mazzanti,
a capillary cobbled street where tired blood
can begin on its way back to the heart,
when he splashed against me in the lobby,
a brass band named Tony from New York,
his autobiography riding on waves of whiskey
breath like the Venus of self-love.
Every year for forty-six years since he chased
the Germans like vermin through these streets
and held a local girl, briefly, in marriage,
he has boomeranged back here, snagged
on the past, baiting the hook
of loneliness with excessive friendliness
in vain against the speechless bodies
riddled with time and the face of a girl
slipping around the corners out of sight.
Then when his desperation implodes,
he bunkers in his room for days,
eyes branching into the red forests
of sleeplessness and the cheap nepenthe
he sucks down, crawling to that last white
door to forgetfulness, the hospital bed.

What I say to him now I say
to myself because I'm not sure
how we can live
past the summer's solstice of our lives,
free from the backward suck of loss,
when each day the sun shatters into stars
and the entire moon of human hope
seems a white tick bloating
on the merely speculated hide of the dark.
As I sit here where my father used to sit

along the Adige, Verona clinging to its curves
like a child to its mother's hips, I
wish I knew how this ancient vein
keeps stepping into its body,
every moment, generation after generation,
without worrying if all that waits is
that coffin of rivers, the heart of water, the sea.

Yet, on certain days I seem to see
a little more with less
like a pupil widening in the dark,
and I wonder now if the high-water mark
of light, the whole brass band of experience,
was to get our utter attention
on the face of this world, the present
tense of being, to follow its long diminuendo
to its dark and lonely center, our senses
refining as we wean from the mother of light
and abandon ourselves to the dark and shine.

THE SPIRIT OF PLACE

Winter's last remnants now thin to white muslin
on the distant blue cones still peaked in snow.
A plane drones overhead while a steady spring warmth
irons nerves to a calm we thought would never come.
New leaves cluster like small green fountains spurting
everywhere from the trees. A slow breeze moves among them
in long whispers like the soft abrasions of air we speak.
The birds outside our five open windows built their nests
last week, their tweezer beaks arriving each time with a pinch
of what will do. Now they persuade intruders away with song,
and white globes speckled with dark stars lie gathered
in the secret woven palms of grass and string.
With so much future present, our winter's passport
longings for Tuscan hills and golden foreign light
seem to have drifted away with the clouds.
Today it seems our best days could be lived anywhere,
maybe, now, even here.

CRABBING

With the land behind us a black rift
between identical shades of blue and
our outboard murmuring its aluminum dream
to ore-laden veins in the earth,
we lift and fall on quiet sighs of water
as it yearns to that center above, the half-moon
like an eye, averted, praying to the East
to lay its naming finger on the world.
We lay our trotline out between buoys—
100 yards of cord stubbed with severed
chicken necks like a crude pearl necklace
offered to the sea, the bloody coil
unravelling behind us from our boat
as something inside us might, snagged
on the world though our breathing dragged us on.
We fasten the other end
and leave time for the enticement of bait,
listening to the green-beige clatter of reeds
that inspired the first musicians
to lash life rafts of panpipes
and give air to their drowning hearts.
We mop our faces and gaze at the seamless weld
of distances we know we will never cross,
trusting the whole sea flows into this finger
of water the way a lover does into his hand
and will give us back at least ourselves
though we come to beg life
from its blood. "Time," my friend says,
and we plow slowly back along the line
which slides like a ridged spine up and over
the plastic-pipe arm clamped to our boatside.
Hooked only on desire, the dreaming sea-spiders follow
to the surface the bitten and sea-blanched necks,

and I web them into this sea too thin for swimming,
dropping them like blue coins into our basket.
At first, as always, there is the clatter of carapace,
of legs skittish above the snapping blue flames,
but soon there reigns an agreement of claws
clamped on claws, on arms, into a face here
and there where lung air bubbles out by an eye.
At first glance they seem joined
in some motionless blue dance, ringed
in a gesture of brotherhood and shared fate
like a universal O of despair. I think
how their basket life seeds a *déjà vu* for tonight
when I will lower them with pincer tongs
into the cauldron, into their last sear of feeling,
and wince, as always, at such drastic love as devouring,
that laying something *other* against our innermost sides
and absorbing all we can through our walls.
But then, as always, I will smile at such sweet white
meat from such a pinching and bottom-feeding world,
my lips burning with the brine of Old Bay,
then numb with cold beer and distilled spirits on ice.

Padre Island

Meaning "father of solitude,"
it's a long brow of sand like a splinter in the sea
where surf breaks and scrapes at the border
in a wrangle of death, a bier of rotting
gull clumps, cracked crabs, and storm-hewn
forests of kelp rimmed in foam. Inland,
among the nerve-nets of vines, the legions of grass
spears, and prickly pears blistered with buds,
it's an old dialogue of dunes:
those waves of sand so slow whole civilizations
of sea oats surf on them for generations
enduring those others, the senseless white broncos,
saddled only by the wind wisping sand off like steam,
stampeding island life with choking drifts
because they have no roots to bind them.
Days burn with the weight of too much light
like too much pain in service of maturation,
bleaching the colors to a sigh, explaining the land,
convincing fresh water to pull up and drift away
until shade is pared to a few gaunt shapes
and faultlines threading through the grass. But
it's among such remnants the mind must harbor itself:
a lizard clutching an oyster chip,
cooling his face in a crack in the sun;
a meadowlark cresting a man-sized knoll,
playing his liquid flute in the splintering wind.

Late Marsh

We must repeat the lessons of the world
from Ptolemaic to Copernican to after that,
finding Heraclitus with his vanished river gone
though we snag downstream after it, years
later, on the same marsh road, tracking
in the bluish sand of evening the weave
of tire ruts unspooling into the distance,
finding swamped trees in leg irons of ice
and herons stranded in wind-rasped ovals
as the pieces of their vision wave away
and daylight's ruining temple falls
in a pillar of gold scimitars across the water
and fades as the sun's red watch
slips into its pocket, leaving
the bruised sky alone to blacken.

PAPER BRIDGE

Sometimes it seems our lives are the childhoods of stars:
the differences, the severances, the expanding from,
building to a place in space.

I think of those who hoard their heart's coinage,
tolling the bridges of flesh arcing toward them
or burning them…

I think of a comet as part of a star's body,
travelling the lonely years, arcing toward another,
a bridge of light like Christ nailing himself to both shores.

I think of you tonight, wherever you are,
high in some glittering constellation. Come down
and stay for awhile, here, on the earth.

PRIMAL SUN, PRIMAL MOON

In those last days of men's belief,
a god must have seen the sun set for the first time,
felt the ground of understanding shift beneath his feet,
watched the eternal light slip down, impossibly down,
then bloody, spill, impale upon the trees,
turning bruise, then black.

We all have some such primal loss,
something we could not bear but did,
something perhaps we have spent our lives
trying to replace or revise.

Maybe that is why we have made so much
of the moon, so many hymns,
because that first stunned night,
opposite where the sun had just died,
something like the sun's blanched face rose,
ghostlike, shining, rescuing the darkness,
the way a loved one's face
or some invented sun
has since climbed into the nights of our lives.

Memory is like that. Memory is moonrise,
both "good" and "bad" (and so is "lunacy"
where the pain is great enough),
and at times when life hurls us downward
or we need to take measure of our lives
and voluntarily climb into the dark,
assenting even if we don't know it to death,
it is the bright wafer we take upon our tongues
in our communion with the night
in order to speak with the light of past days,
saying "I remember, I re-member,"

and so rejoin the dismembered body of our experience
with thought, in a fullness
greater than present time or loss or confusion,
and in the end we may,
with a few persons who have labored long
in the fields of memory, not only reflect,
but radiate with the received light of our world.

FROM *Eulogy for a Private Man*

WORDS FOR A PERFECT EVENING

Even a perfect evening eventually yawns
and goes to sleep to awaken changed in the morning.
Each day must be wrestled for beauty among

this permanent impermanence where clouds shift their shape
in the shifting wind and the sudden blossomings of illness,
the carcinomas in the brain, change the possible

future to a river's mouth widening at the sea's edge.
And yet there is a durability here,
lives that somehow replenish themselves

around a center in the gravity of affection, the way
the earth turns itself to be touched everywhere
by the light. What else can I say to you tonight,

that meaning is the wine we press from the context we share,
that our daily devotion depends on a presence and absence,
on arms that gather the invisible flowers we find

growing among our ruins, and arms that bear
nothing but a guarded emptiness, a space preserved,
a dependable harbor waiting for someone we love.

THE FIRE

When I was a child, the elderly frightened me.
They were the withered ones near death. Their faces
shriveled around their skulls like prunes on pits.

All the rivers of the world had gouged their skin,
and their spidery legs were webbed with bruised veins.
Once, a woman's watering eyes glared

at me with pools of fire, and I saw myself
reflected there like a fly stuck in that burning.
But now, my body's singing stutters in pain,

and the waterways of time sculpt my face.
The web tightens its net. The future shrinks,
but each moment swells with a fullness of past

I never could have guessed. I imagine an end
so sated with life that I drop out of time
like ripe fruit to the earth. I imagine

a moment so wide that I spread from my body
and embrace everything like the sky.
But lullabies are easy in times of peace,

and lately I search the eyes of the old for the white
burn of a mind defying the body's betrayals,
for a humor and kindness free among the ruins,

for a glimpse of spirit beneath the flesh that sloughs
like velvet on antlers, a spirit *almost visible*,
chiseled with pain, tempered in the fire of this world.

Revelations

Nostalgia for the future beyond
the black wall eclipsed his path.
The earth grew heavy within him and wanted

to sleep. The days no longer buttoned
inside the uniforms of order.
The streams of desire ran dry in their beds.

The light could see no point in staying.
Others around him were looting their lives,
minting children, painting self-portraits

for the coffers of art, or carving sepulchers
of fame to lie in memory forever.
The cairns of despair were everywhere.

Elegies filled the air. But then
he thought how little we live our lives,
how the black wall was a black angel

pointing us back to the moment we have,

to the one grain in the eye of the hourglass,
to the one altar of sacrifice,
to even the moment the heart must fist

to existence and hammer the point of being
like a nail, to even the moment so painful
the mind wants to leap from its fire,

to even the blue cold moment
in caterpillar days that crawl
through the long winters--all must be lived

so endurance can bear its revelation,
and the fist ease to an open palm,
and the fire quench in a time of water,

and the blue turn as rose as the blue
newborn that gasps its first breath
and its two lungs billow like sails.

In the Season of Memory

Still, we have this fear of coming to nothing,
of clutching the years at the end like a cluster of stalks,
the long dry flowerless stems of thought,
the deeds leading to dead-end alleys,
leaving not one star-point of meaning
to shine above our sleep in someone's night.

For a brief season of memory our name may be
a berry of sadness sweet on a tongue that speaks it,
a rinse of rain clearing an ear that hears it,
but will there still be time, even at the end,
for some essential drop of mind to spread
like dye momentarily through the clarity of time
or burst like a bubble on a rain-pummeled pond
with some brief scent of individual air?

If only we could be like the stars when they die,
their final explosions of light like death-blossoms
seeding new matter in the fertile night.

Sunday Evening

I.

"Death is also the *thief* of beauty," he says,
as a slow disquietude replaces morning's calm.
The pink light fades from ashen clouds,
and an icy luminosity begins to wax
above the highlands of eternity.
The willow, weeping all evening over rocks
beside the pond, darkens to an arch hunched
above a wafer of sacramental light,
a fallen moon too faint to give much sight.
There were minds which might have ripened into suns
had not the body failed, the nursing vine
sallowed and withered before the fruit was ripe.
We are flowers of light in a field of darkness,
brief in our pulse of generations. We open
and close, wax and wane, open and close.

II.

Death of the body is not the only death.
Our seasons of loss prepare us for the end,
the gardens withered in droughts of circumstance,
the taut and cold receding lips of love,
the glance that lowers and turns away forever,
the fires of hope snuffed by the winds of change
on the ledges above, the dim glitter of stars
in the pond's eye like distant citadels
we'll never know but we had once lived by.
Death of the body is not the only death.
A winter mind that never turns to spring
has had too much of suffering. Its crystal eyes
no longer see the colors of our lives.
An empty house collapses under snow
in whiteness cleansed of feeling long ago.

III.

Where are the stars of death in the pointed night?
Is it sacrilege or only emulation
to want to be a god? A brazen boy
flings against the Goliaths of circumstance,
his sling, a frayed genetic rope he weaves
to the furthest nebulae at the end of thought,
a human tree whose height might reach eternity.
The fire-feathered bird among its branches
sings a human song on the edge of space.
It beckons through the rocks of time and place.
It sings of fire and ice, but not of death.
It sings of seasons and dreams, but not of death.
An ancient king who lingers on his throne
hears its song and dreams of wanderings,
of odysseys among the distant stars.

The Force of Intent

At times we force our destiny like rivers
carving canyons to the sea or trees
that crack the rocks they wedge to reach the light.

But the politics of will depend on change,
the force of our intent in *circumstance*.
How easily we trample the green havens,

dissolve chapels of mist in scorching light.
How quickly we bridle at roadblocks and chasms
and turn from the philosophy of lakes.

But our certainties are destined for revision
like morning maps of an evening land. We know
at last the mountains are more than we supposed,

and our wagons sit stranded by snow in the pass.
The yellow pride of noon turns blue at dusk.
The walking boy becomes the wheelchair man.

THE MAN AND THE CEMETERY EFFIGY

The years of failure had wounded his hope beyond
recovery. The erotic postures of possible futures
no longer duped him. His path closed.

Each evening he watched the drape of light
dissolve as night disrobed. At noon he knew
the nakedness of darkness. He stood on the ice of time

waiting to fall through. Then one night
he wandered like a homeless drunk in the cemetery
among the black flames of the trees, the whispering

leaves, the moonlit stones in rows like teeth
with nothing but the sky to bite against,
and there he found the black angel spreading

its wings of despair like a wall eclipsing the stars,
and he knelt in nausea to receive its benediction
and was told to find his freedom in hopelessness,

to find his dignity in obscurity, and to root
his life among the dead where even those
who would be gods eventually grow human.

WORDS

I do not speak of certain things.
All talk would be the scuffed air

we shovel over the dead. Sometimes
the air is a grave on which no words

will tread, and language stands speechless
on the edge, vivid with silence.

But sometimes words are the only hands
we have to touch a bruised memory

or cleanse a wound that never healed
or lift a body we've carried for years

at last to the pyre of shared grief.
I remember a dying girl, lying

curled in dust, flies on her lips
and eyes, her swollen belly pregnant

with death. I remember her soft, struggling
breath and the hum of flies in the quiet heat.

LETTER TO A FRIEND

Who knows what age will bring besides your death?
You think you see your future plod before you,
eventless, a blunt-toothed cog of certainty,

churning for years of noon in summer heat,
but haven't there been times when suddenly you saw
something which had been there all along

and nothing had changed but you, a certain slant
of age, perhaps, or disposition of the eyes,
some newfound sensitivity, awakened when

adversity scraped the skin of your perception?
The starving leaves now blaze with colors
not seen until articulated by the frost.

These years of erosion may yet uncover forgotten
ruins--your own, standing there like a child,
holding out the key to your next room.

The Past

The "nameless unremembered acts of kindness"
are never lost. They whisper to our dreams

like a mother's hum on the distant edge of sleep.
They are the ghosts of benevolence whose many

unseen hands lift us in seasons of pain
and lead us to chapels of faith in the stained glass

of our perceptions. Their influence is always there,
the way the stars are always there, even

in day, the distant suns of times past
mixing their light with the bright noon of the present.

The Gift

When we arrive bodiless with only our memories,
will we have loved life enough to paint
its face in light on the black page of eternity?

When our bodies are torn open like envelopes,
what news will our ancestors be able to read in us?
Will we have gathered just a little more

than they, be able to offer some nuance of feeling
or subtlety of perception they had missed,
or at least bear a glow to nurse their nostalgia

and lighten their darkening? Or will we have lived
in vain and fail even to reach the past
which waits ahead gravely with open arms,

fail even to recognize their faces
which then will turn from us, stranding us
like feeble stars in the dark space of ignorance?

THE GLOWING COAL

As he had feared, the world was going to end
sooner than expected. The future now
narrowed to months. He stepped outside.

A haze had lifted he had not known was there.
Edges of things seemed sharp enough to cut.
The world glittered. He stood inside a diamond.

So much had been held back, so much to spend.
He felt a sudden love for everything,
even the moldering garbage at his feet.

Each swirl and eddy of the world, each smell,
flavor, hue, touch, and tone would now
burn inside the flame of his attention.

He would not lapse, even inside his pain.
If only this coal he carried to the darkness
would somehow take eternity to fade.

Transitory Music

Each Sunday he'd go with his family
up the stony lane to the church,
its gray stones mortared tight,
its windows plain as daylight,
its one steeple like a blunt thorn
scratching cries from the invisible wind.
They'd all be there: the bored deadbeats,
the sleepy obligated children,
the worn seeking peace, the mournful
and frightened laying their pain on the altar
of belief, the cheery pews of hopefuls
planting themselves in rows like bulbs,
the reverent who had almost grown mute.

Some days he'd almost join the leafless
trees in pleading with the sky,
but he knew he would squander eternity,
having only lived a few
moments of his life. A moment
fully lived, he thought, would be like air
embracing everything that is.
He kept breathing past redemption,
though sometimes he heard a music
scratched into being by the thorns of experience
and stood inside the stained light
and felt the rose open, the fist
unclench its five fingers of sense,
and he carried an open hand
for as long as he could into the world.

The Unlived

If only he could memorize like a lover
the body of the ordinary, which was already
a dream much larger than all sleep.

He regretted the future—the one he *would* have lived—
the way he regretted the past, the fossil record
of mere fact, the life that died into being

while all the unlived possibilities
echoed into silence among the vaulted
arches and stained glass rosettes of time.

Each day was proof of his failure to flare
into ash at the flashpoint of recognition
or crack ecstatically open in the globed moment,

saving nothing for his next breath. How easily
his imagination yawned and slept, how vision
grew young and frolicked in the shallows of perception.

His mind floated like a sponge in an ocean, soaked
full by a mere palmful of water, immersed
in all that it would never come to know.

PLANES

The season of heat had passed.
Rain had deepened the dust
with umber and raw sienna.

Houses had gathered inward
there on the treeless hill.
He heard two voices pass

and the clopple of horses on cobbles
fade out of reach. The street
began to fill with mist,

which drifted from the valley below
as if searching for something...a way
to give itself a shape,

some form among the forms.
It drifted from house to house,
pressing its wet face

against the nearly invisible
planes of the windowpanes,
baffled it could not go

where it could see—places
he would never be
and never know why.

There was something about
the matter of his domain,
the density of his life.

AT THE GRAND CANYON

Clouds float like islands in the river of air
which flows between the walls. The Colorado,

a sliver of water, glints at the bottom like a knife.
Ephemeral as fruit flies, airplanes flit

among the cliffs, while laden mules labor
down to a present millions of years below.

On the edge of the gouge, herds of awed tourists
gape at the immense ruined rainbows of time.

"I wish we could live here," someone says,
not noticing the clutch of desert plants

struggling at his feet, which soon will die
and blow across the stones, stain the rocks,

or lodge as molecules of dust in someone's eye.
How much grandeur does it take until

our eyes fall to the small life before us,
the geologic blink we call our lives,

how long before we settle on a few roots
finding life in a handful of burning sand,

keeping their grip inside the wind which whistles
faintly as it whets against their limbs.

Letter to Genetically Engineered Super Humans

You are the children of our fantasies of form,
our wish to carve a larger cave of light,
our dream to perfect the ladder of genes and climb

its rungs to the height of human possibility,
to a stellar efflorescence beyond all injury
and disease, with minds as bright as newborn suns

and bodies which leave our breathless mirrors stunned.
Forgive us if we failed to imagine your loneliness
in the midst of all that ordinary excellence,

if we failed to understand how much harder
it would be to build the bridge of love
between such splendid selves, to find the path

of humility among the labyrinth of your abilities,
to be refreshed without forgetfulness,
and weave community without the threads of need.

Forgive us if you must re-invent our flaws
because we failed to guess the simple fact
that the best lives must be less than perfect.

THE BODILY BEAUTIFUL

Ah, the bodily beautiful, how they are envied
for the perfect rhymes of their bodies' moons and stars,
how the world sets sail for the labial latitudes
of their lustrous skin, forgetting the bloody factories

within. But what of their burden? the daily swelter
in the spotlights of lust, the lovesick legions
and crush of attentive puppets, the ceaseless chatter
and charades of mating games, the splatter of night-

frightened moths who fling against their panes.
How hard it must be among fiestas
of permission and satin pillows to practice forbearance
and cleanse the spirit in the deserts of self-denial,

how hard to leave the shallows of sexuality
and immerse in the treacherous waters of love, to glimpse
the skull of time in the mirror's lie and the bones
of honesty inside those sublime impediments of flesh.

The Woman with Gravitas

There's nothing now she wants or needs from us.
A sad and liquid peace has filled her eyes.

The wreckage of her life has massed inside her,
the way the dust of stars now forms the earth.

The weight of her despair outweighs the world,
so all things bend or fall towards her center.

Children climb into the safety of her arms.
Men and women orbit her like moons.

She seldom speaks, but smiles and listens patiently.
She moves inside a weather of her own

like an evening star which seems to grow more bright
the more it grows immersed inside the night.

EULOGY FOR A PRIVATE MAN

He would not arrange his face to please us,
smile on cue or chime with ritual greeting,
would not distill himself into an aperitif,

dance or fence or wrestle with clever speech,
add to the litter of words that silence sweeps.
He was a dry stream, flowing unseen beneath

his arid bed, a social counterweight
to the harlequins of humid revelation.
But sometimes a lean, muscular sentence would stride

before us and cross its arms in a stubborn stance,
then turn away, as if remembering how the flimsy
bridges we fling to span the abyss collapse,

how our strings of meaning unravel as we speak.
He annoyed us and intrigued us, a hieroglyph
of cliff-faced solitude we tried to decipher.

But perhaps such a stern gravity was necessary
to keep his secret wild moons circling,
or perhaps he preferred the untrammelled woods

of his loneliness and reserved it as a private garden
for one who never came, or perhaps some eclipse
of love produced an arctic cold, a sentinel

trusting no one at the gate, or perhaps
he kept a monstrous rage inside his torment
which could not lapse for one mauled moment.

Who knows the terms of another's life? For some
it may be a victory even to achieve
a distant closeness, an intimate alienation.

In the Humid Zone

No doubt we should garden our emotions,
pull the weeds of misanthropy, build the bridges
of affection and understanding where we can,

prod ourselves to leave our comfort zones
and our gazing through the windowpanes of books.
No doubt we should find our way outside

among the grid of streets and scabs of concrete,
among the herds of humid personalities,
the brushfires of contention, the abrasive crudity,

the social pirates, the webs of intrigue,
the conquerors who try to colonize our minds,
the sledgehammers and foghorns of opinion

whose statements drop to the floor and gather flies,
the cloying hormones, the drones of mincing minds.
No doubt we should suffer this swelter

if only to be reminded of our unperfected
patience, our small forgiveness, the great growth
still required of our insufficient love.

Dissertation on Dogs

Your basic dog, you see, is your basic animal.
Untrained, it seems a comical and vulgar creature,
a kind of raging id which lacks all continence.

It pushes through the world teeth-first
like a machine whose mission is solely eating meat.
It masticates manure and licks itself in public!

Its tongue hangs and pants and drools, and its nose
is wantonly wet for every pollen of scent.
In short, it's a wonder dogs are commonly sought as pets.

Yet, there are many things to recommend them.
We share a kinship with the dog, expressed
in certain phrases such as "I'm howlin' for you

darlin'" or "I'm hot on the trail of *love*,"
and on dog days in this dog eat dog world,
when the warp and woof of our companionship

grows thin, we find a certain friend in the dog,
a kind of caninical law of unswerving loyalty.
We find a fluency in those sympathetic eyes,

the sorrowful stares, the brow-lifts of concern,
and in the tail, a barometer of anger and fear,
a metronome of pleasure thumping on the floor,

and in the voice, a whimper or staccato of pain,
the hatchet blows of obsession, the sirens of yearning,
a forlorn and arctic loneliness to match our own.

In fact, in the presence of such spirituality,
we may wonder if a dog-*soul* exists or merely
an epiphenomenon of canine-mind, a flower

of spirit which wilts when the root of flesh is cut.
This question further taunts us when we note
a comportment of restraint in an *old* dog, an economy

of wag, an air of wisdom in the graying at the eyes,
and a meditative posture readily assumed
when the nose rests on paws in an attitude of prayer.

In summation, I leave you with this question:

could they be some higher form, visiting disguised,
say lovable angels who lower themselves to train us
in the purity, fidelity, and art of adoration?

EXPEDITIONS OF A MISANTHROPE

Whenever he safaried to the jungle swirl,
the gadflies goaded. The vines of alliance curled

their tendrils of obligation around his limbs.
The piranhas, schooled, waited for him to swim.

The parrots chattered. The snakes slithered in pits.
The monkeys grabbed each other's tails and pinched.

The wolves and vultures circled mating pairs.
The macaws displayed their scarlet feathers for a fare.

The lions and hyenas mawled the bleating meek.
The rats crawled in fecal mass and reeked.

He always left, wondering why he came
so unpracticed and unwilling to play in jungle games.

In the Absence of Rain

Here our sacred ground is cracked with drought.
Poverty whispers like a saw. Clouds pass
as if this rift of dust did not exist.
Our poems call down the rain, but the measured

furrows wait. Our philosophies of pain
are the thin music we drape over silence.
Each day the ruse of possibility
is harder to maintain. The years deepen

the unread lines in the cliff's face. Shall
we mutter restlessly among the white hills
or sit listless in the fields, deformed
by necessity, like the wind-blasted pines

whose branches all trail on one side?
Or shall we give one great sigh,
one great lapse of flesh, and leave
our petitionless bones lying on the miserly earth?

CHAINS OF CHANGE

In drought the mind clouds with humid visions,
and in cold seas we sail for the islands of summer
where pink roses of pleasure petal open

and fall in fleshy haloes on the grass. Serenity
waits for us in the green silence after
love, in the aftertaste of wine, in the heaven

where we imagine we could linger forever.
But desire gathers on the boundaries of difference
like droplets on a cold glass in warm air,

and when the sparkling moment eventually warms
to the general mood, the dew steams back
to its former self, drifting toward some

new island in time. Aren't we like that?
Wouldn't the long incarcerations in happiness
leave us longing for sadness, praying for a few

flames to singe our ease, for archipelagoes
of pain to erupt in our seas of content as reasons
for sailing, as the indispensable linkage of our lives.

MIGRATORY FLIGHT

We could deny our winters, refuse to cut
our hands mining the sharp ores of grief.
Whenever the cold comes, we could follow

the arrowheads of geese shafting south
to an azure place where whales sing offshore
and otters frolic in the wanton surf.

We could grow soft as children in the arms
of leisure, but we might never learn in time
how to stoke the cold fire of the will

in that winter we cannot refuse, when we must glean
from the icy fields the last scattered grains
we once disdained, with only the luminous pallor

of the moon scarfed in clouds to light our way,
rising above the outstretched arms of the trees
in its long slow journey through the night.

Dido

When he left to plow the sea and husband
other lands, she became all fire.
Her frenzied flames clutched at air. Smoke

coiled over the city and frayed among
the clouds and seaward wind. Her soul weighed
on the pyre and plunged beneath the embers,

thrusting deep into the dark like a root
to the waters of misery. She wandered in woods,
in wastelands and night, robed in the fire

of new arrivals. Others who had darkened
inside their cloaks withdrew from her
like ships among the trees. Her form glared

through the woods. Her stares scorched all
they tried to hold. The littering leaves
burned beneath her feet. She sought the nets

of branches, but none could hold her close enough.
She could not find the swamp to douse herself
inside its pools or find the river to drown

herself inside its embrace. So she wandered,
a fire wrapped in fire. Once, he came,
pleading, armored, but she had considered

the nature of ships, the loading and unloading,
the angling of sails for wind, considered
the nature of harbors, open for whatever

sea-weary fates come sailing in.
And so, her ears were closed when he spoke
as if from underwater on the sea's bed.

She choked her words before they could be born,
then clenched inside her fire and wrenched away.
But after that turning inward, she changed.

At first, desire dulling to despair, she started
to darken like the rest, but then no longer
wandered the woods: she stood among the trees,

discerning the shades of shade, the way
loneliness shifted into solitude.
Her glances lingered with understanding,

which frightened many at first, and tremors of speech
rumbled through the silence in that region.
She lightened as the heavy blood of self

drained from her fire, and saffron dawn
welled from the fissure in her chest, spreading
across her soul. She smiled, listening to those

who came to her, consoling them as they took
her light. A glow lingered wherever
she walked. The fragrance of her compassion

incensed the dark. Faces emerged from cowls
and shone, reflecting her affection. Legions
gathered, illumined, a pale and fallen heaven.

There was talk of eviction and further punishment.
The Light and Dark sparked in correspondence.
But in the end, Hell decided it wanted her there

to feed the flames of the damned. Her kindness
would fester as their greatest points of pain,
the seeds of heaven they could never gain.

And Heaven too required that she stay
to show all souls how miracles grow from misery
like roses growing from a bed of glowing coals.

THE REHEARSAL

Somewhere else there is someone who will never
die. Somewhere else the moonlight washes
the bodies of lovers with milk, nursing their dreams.

Here, the windows suffocate in drapes.
Shadows frieze on the wall. I lie in the heat,
unable to close my eyes, rehearsing myself

for the end, knowing my slot in time will soon
clot with darkness and the last dirt will drum
on my box of borrowed earth. I rehearse

for the time I will choke in a world of air and claw
like a swimmer sinking to the sea's floor. How
will I compose myself, what song will I

have practiced enough to quiet the terrors of hell?
I search the expensive years for a secret rain,
a white noise, a curtain of inner light

I can draw around myself like a shroud.
I walk back through the years, searching
the layers of golden light and dried blood,

all the way back to the black door
before birth where I practice stepping through,
knowing this time it is only a beginning.

The Last Voyage

On nights like this, how clear
the moonlight is, anointing trees
hushed by the water's edge with light
floating on the surface of their leaves.

I think of Crane at the end, slipping
into the dark sea, abandoning everybody,
all bridges down but one,
swimming towards Belle Isle,

his own unbetrayable reply.
Was it like that those last moments
when he grew tired of correspondences
and the flagless piracy of critics, thinking

no deeds but words, no words but deeds,
fulfilling his own prophecy?
I imagine it differently.
This time he floats, a splintered seer,

in the cool Caribbean brine, refusing
the lifesavers tossed to him
like oo many hands reaching
into his solitude. This time

the passengers crowd the rail and stare
in disbelief as he, rising
and swelling, watches them crate away,
their bright lights shrinking from sight—

a glowing egg, then a star, then night.
Not all endings are a failure
of the imagination to go on.
There is a sea-change of heart

in the dark waters of this version,
a sudden liberation wanting at the last
what maybe was wanted from the start—
not transport, but immersion.

The Four Rings

NEW POEMS

interdependent rings of relationship:
self, family, community, divinity

THAT DAY

All day the cold rain fell, its clear bloodless beads
shattering all around us as if legions of angels
were dropping their rosaries, abandoning prayer.

STOPPING AT A T-INTERSECTION IN LATE AUTUMN

At a stop sign on a country road,
I pull to the side, turn my headlights
and engine off, and listen to the quiet
as sunset's embers whisper on the hearth's horizon.
Reddened cloud-clumps darken to bruise
as the blues deepen in last light. Trees,
leafless, print their line of hieroglyphs
against the smoldering sky. *What do they say?*
I wonder, as I have always wondered.
I know that heartwood lies at the center of each,
wrapped in rings from years of silent reaching,
and I see now that my road ends here,
here at the side of another. Why should I turn
west or east? Warming myself in last light,
I am amazed that at the heart of things,
a child swaddled in years is content to go nowhere,
rocking in place, rocking to sleep,
on the edge of eternity.

THE MOMENT

When you are waiting in the vestibule
of eternity, and your name is called,

and your last terror begins, as it will,
and your body starts to close like a darkening house,

what memory will you summon from the book of stains,
what moment that you loved *so much*

that, even in the final trembling, you can hold its vision
until you step inside its presence, forever.

The Blue Whale

Our five-year-old daughter bubbles with laughter
as she bounces on her bed, pure joy flashing
in her eyes like the glint of fingerlings in sunlit waves.
Tired now, she settles happily between us to read
a bedtime book about blue whales, far offshore,
singing in the open sea. We learn they are
the largest animals on earth, but only feed
on the smallest things. As we lie on her bed, we notice the small
lashed crescents of her eyelids begin to settle together
like the evening sky closing against the horizon.
We smile at one another, turn lights out, and crescent
our bodies around her like two hands closing in prayer.
We are teaching our daughter to trust the darkness enough
to sleep, so tonight we pretend her bed is a raft,
floating on the sea, while crickets somehow sing outside
our window in the moonlit grass. As she slowly drifts
to sleep, still sucking her thumb, we watch as the rise and fall
of her breath begins to slow and she dreams on the swells of time.
One more time this evening we find ourselves
in this space we make at the end of our days, so we stay
for awhile in the eternal moment, then place two pillows
where our bodies were and wade up the hallway
to our marriage bed, too tired to do much more than lie
on our love raft and whisper a few good words.
Times were, we lived so much for the future that hope
was a thief in our home. All the small things went missing.
But teaching this child we are learning to trust the rise
and fall of our days. We know the unspeakable
grief that lies ahead, and so as we drift to sleep
on our bed, our bodies gently tethered by our embrace,
I imagine we are all gathered together
into one blue being the color of evening, surrounded
by small glittering things as plentiful as stars,
as we sing and float in the vast expanse of time, forever.

THE GENTLE FIRE

Sunday morning, on a trail inside the Smoky Mountains,
my daughter and I see dozens of swallowtail butterflies
gathered on the ground and swirling in the air
like breeze-stirred leaves.   The sun-yellow wings
of the males seem to blaze against the rain-darkened earth
and hues of forest green, as they mix with the glimmering
midnight-blues of the females. They lift and settle
as they jostle to sip the water from a mud-puddle's edge.
Then they rise to travel just a wing-beat away
to feed on fresh snail-crush among the boot-crunched gravel.

They make a strange and gentle fire, these wing-flames,
sun-yellow and night-dark, lifting and falling
between the mud's water and the snail-body's mud.

My daughter, now in butterfly-light, enters among them
and tries to coax a pair of wings onto her finger,
her shining pink-white hand lifting and falling
among the fluttering possibilities. At last, a yellow flame
descends and settles on her finger-branch, and for one
eternal moment, he opens a pair of stained-glass windows
for her gaze before he lifts away. My daughter, radiant,
turns to me and whispers, and a lightness lifts inside me,
as she settles her hand into my hand,
and her dark eyes lift to me, filled with light.

"Why? Why Not?"

My daughter asks. I do not want to frighten her—
too much too soon is like a hard rain
that runs right off our hills and floods.
I search for words that she can carry
like lanterns when I'm gone. I want to say
"Be careful—each moment seeds our future" or
"Our gardens are decisions that must be tended
or their character is lost." I want to warn that
even little things can gather like a film on glass
and dim our view of life until the darkness
opens up inside us like a pit.
But I only say what satisfies for now,
and hope these years are centered in her
like a hearth where she can go throughout her life
to shelter from the cold, and hear the murmur
of her father's voice, whispering in warm tones.

CHILDREN AND DEATH

Procreation presupposes death,
but I had never been consoled by this
or that the ancient tree is kept alive
only by dropping its blighted and bitten leaves.
The real thing was always impossible,
the body on the bed, flat and still,
the heaviness of clay in the last embrace.

All that changed when she was born
as snow is changed, falling in the sea.
I'd lose it all to keep her safe—
clear lakes on summer days,
wine and food in maple shade,
mountain paths, forest mists,
fireflies, frost-limned leaves,
the stars, the planets not yet seen—
all.
        When I first saw her bud
of light—gentle, innocent, helpless,
shining as if the essence of the world
were glowing through her skin—
I entered a room where I had never been
and Self dissolved. I knew then I must give
my life in this windy world to cup around
her flame, whose life could only live if loved.
There are reasons we find beyond the self.

THE MIGRANT COUPLE

After long hours of mindless labor,
yoked with debt, they are released like oxen

to graze in the remnant grass of another day.
Some evenings a glance or thawing touch

is all it takes for affection to stream like light
into their dark mood, but other times they scald

the air with angry talk or burrow in silence
until the inedible dirt in their throats loosens.

One of them may have to pour for hours
the carefully balanced words they've cellared like wine

before the other can unclench and enter the inner
room of intimacy, shedding the heavy clothes

the self wears in the world's weather. But then
the ordinary fare of daily living begins

to fill their evening, like a soundless hymn they sing
between them in the chamber of their private life,

They linger in the mornings and then begin, again.

LA FARGE: ENTRANCE TO THE TAUTIRA RIVER, TAHITI, *FISHERMAN SPEARING A FISH*

This sky-glazed water, hedged by mountains,
lies so still that it could be the amniotic lake
where the river begins or the calm mouth
of the river's end. It's hard to say
with everything pastel, serene, and held at bay.
Even the clouds are as motionless as islands.
A woman stands on the water's edge
with her arms crossed as she watches the man
in the mirroring shallows poised with a spear.
His tanned body is taut as a drawn bow.
They are already a river, the man and the woman,
and if his aim is good, he may claim enough
from the other side of the reflection to sustain them
one more day. But this is still that time between times
when one moment lies waiting for the pierce of the next
to send it streaming. We frame it inside our yearning,
an eternal beginning we point ourselves towards, reflecting,
but flowing beside it, flowing past it, unable to stay.

The Birth of Don Juan

The others have it wrong. Before he was "Don Juan,"
he was only a young man in love with a girl
who used to walk along the shore with him and talk.
Then, one day, they sought shelter from the wind
and rain in a cave, built a fire between them, and stayed.

Love is like a white bird   that flies above an inland sea
*   in the whitest calm   of the clearest sky*
and keeps on flying   as long as each wing is true.

We'll never know why she left for the Marquis,
a man so poor he only had money, but whatever the reason,
she settled on the leeward side of love and left
poor Juan bereft. He did not know that the Dawn of Love
is entered only once, and for years went door to door
with a key that fit all locks but his own. Until the end,
when his latest conquest failed him, his eyes
would glaze and gaze inland, where he still walked
with her, hand in hand, beside a glittering sea.

JAPANESE SCREEN

A red bridge arches
        across a black stream. Willows
            fall in green fountains.

                On the stream's bed, trout
                    slide among globed stones rubbed smooth
                        by the seaward flow.

                Women with baskets
            rest among tree roots, their gnarled
        knuckles caked with earth.

        Workers in loin cloths
    glisten with sweat, their only
shade under their hats.

A beggar, soaking
        in urine and vomit, yearns
            for the clink of coins.

                Servants, lifting men
                    in chairs, bend backs like bows that
                      soon will spring or crack.

                  Nightside, moonlit trees
                hang green screens around lovers
            whose skins gleam like milk.

        Near, nervous horses
    snort and stamp. Dogs bark. A thief
scurries like a roach.

In a dim lit street,
        a woman is bought. Hands crawl
            like flies on her hips.

            A girl's silk dress shines
                in a courtyard, a lantern
                    men circle like moths.

                  East, a mother feeds
              her child as trees drop petals
        in her streaming hair.

      Azaleas, clustered
   like butterflies on sticks, ring
themselves with pink moats.

Spring-swollen streams fall
        from cliffs, split on rocks, thread down,
           and branch into roots.

            South, men bend to scythe
                hay, piling sheaves in stubble
                    where grasshoppers cling.

                  Insects hum in weeds.
              Boats float down slow rivers. Haze
        hides the mountain's peak.

      An iron bell clangs,
   shaking like a bloom in wind.
The air clears for prayer.

West, in blood-stained fields,
          grass curls around rocks. Dry stalks
                    rattle in the wind.

                    Blots of dead horses
                              dot the valley's fields, their eyes
                                        staring, glazed with sky.

                              Soldiers bloat in heat.
                    Their tight skins thrum with maggots
          churning to make wings.

          North, above the peak's
     snow-cloaked shoulder, the moon peers,
pale as the sun's ghost.

Footprints track across
          winter fields, cups of darkness
                    leading through the snow.

                    Below, iced trees cast
                              their river nets in darkness:
                                        white-veined bloodshot eyes.

PORTRAITS OF MY SON AS A YOUNG BOY

I.   West of Eden

Childhood is the springtime of humanity,
the eternal Eden through which we're forced to pass,
which is why, perhaps, even frozen adults
in the presence of children may thaw into smiles,
restored for a while to their own first days
when happiness came easy and even rage
was pure and brief like a harmless summer squall
at sea.
           And so my son, even on the hardest days,
dazzles me, as he flowers in my gaze—as all children
flower when looked upon with love.

He is a redbud bursting from a winter branch.
He is a yellow crocus thrusting through the snow.
Joy-light wells inside him. His skin glows.

Laughing-eyes, wind-racer, he surges with the force
of Life, as yet undimmed by our shadows and strife.

I guard the borders of his land, the flaming
sword of knowledge heavy in my hand.

II.   Café

My son is prickly as a grouchy king today.
His little hand is wrapped around my finger
as he pulls and screams annoyance with
our errands. Toddler-swagger, loaded diaper,
he only needs a scepter. Our sidewalk leads
us past the café crowd at little tables,

preoccupied with cell phones, laptops, lattes,
until my son, Italian tenor, hits
his high note of displeasure, and then they turn
their dagger eyes to fix on him
as if a cockroach crawled on their croissants.
How dare my son disrupt the greatest story
ever told—their own. I lift my head, return
their glare as if a lion father sniffed hyenas
in the air, then usher the King away,
his sanctity still screaming in my ears.

III.   After Picking Up My Son from Kindergarten

"The child is father of the man," the great Bard said,
and sometimes father of the father, I might add.

We were in the car today and stuck in traffic
as it rained. "Dad, Dad," he said breathlessly,
as if he'd run from a distant village with an urgent message.
"Look, rain snakes!" he said, pointing to his window
where raindrop runnels wriggled down head-first.
And then, before I'd had a chance to marvel at
my little Bard of the Children's Garden, he quickly pointed
outside and said, "The rainbow's like a big feather!"
Then I thought about a giant bird of light as we sat
at another traffic light.
                              After that, at home,
he showed me art he'd drawn at school. I asked him why
the water had an eye and all the trees were yellow.
He replied, "Because the stream is looking at me
and my teacher said the trees eat light."
                              My son,
you are a spring rain rinsing my dusted sight.
You awaken my habit-eyes that have learned to sleep.
Your life is poetry. Take my hand. Lead me to your lands.

THE DIVERS

This pool, though only chorine-pure, is much preferred
to the rock ledge and bile-green water of the quarry outside town
with its algal rafts and snakes and submerged logs
which can dislodge and rise at any time.
So, on these cloud-fluffed summer days,
they commune here for relief from the heat and to master
the dive, to practice springing from the boards to the air
so they may fall in their own way to the sky-blue box
of water waiting beneath. The children train to plunge
head-first, making a steeple of their arms so their bodies
slide painlessly in. They learn it's all about style,
this entering the water. Miss your angle and you will sting
at the change in density; miss your time and you may slap
flat on your back as if stunned on concrete. But beyond that,
what draws them up these ladders is greater than fear:
it's a certain joy in perfecting the body's expression
on its way to total immersion: watch the time-defying
somersaults and twists crammed into split seconds,
watch the arched cross of the swan as it lunges face-first
into space, watch the quick click of the jack knife as it opens
and slips through the slit it cuts in the water's skin,
watch even the graceless cannonball, that anarchic favorite
of the young, which requires a certain skill to rise high
above the earth in a tight fetal curl and plummet so hard
you pock the pool like a meteor and douse the self-anointing
chaise-lounge crowd with a crater-edge of spray.
Ah, dear divers, these are good days and may they stay with you,
may they soak so thoroughly in that when you stand someday
on that jagged ledge above the pit of dark water, you will open
your arms to embrace it all or steeple yourself into hope
or roll yourself into a ball of experience, a world, globed,
and ready to lodge in that denser sphere of what is.

INDEPENDENCE DAY

This afternoon my daughter and I released the ant-farm ants
among the flowers in our garden. They had been sandwiched
between clear plastic walls so we could watch them tunnel
through some green translucent goo the factory sent
that served as soil and food. It didn't seem right,
so we removed the roof from their slice of world
and let them crawl to the greater world of soil crumbs, leaf-mold,
and forests of flower stalks. I doubt if they thought
of the hands that freed them, but we freed them anyway.

Tonight, outside, we join thousands of other people
crawling the streets to watch the fireworks display.
My daughter rides my shoulders so she can see
beyond the tall stalks of strangers in our garden of humanity.
She is clearly the flower of my life,
and so my hands hold tight onto her legs so she does not fall,
while she watches in awe the giant stalks of sparks that sizzle
suddenly upwards in the night and burst overhead
into blossoms of light, dazzles of red, white, blue, gold, and green.

I think of all the sacrifice it took and seems to take
to flower into peace, how even now there are hands unseen
that guard this crowd, and legions of soldier-cells that scour
our inner shores for furtive microbes that oar
in darkness up our streams. What a rhyme
of circumstance it takes to hold our time,
but in the thin slice of time I have,
sandwiched between this dark soil and black sky,
I hold my daughter's life as best I can.
I know I must release her soon
to the greater world beyond my life,
to flower in the dark night beyond my last thought,
but for the time, being, we are here together, free enough
with space enough for a father's love and a child's delight
in a brief season of fire-flowers in a dark garden of light.

MAKING SOAP BUBBLES WITH MY DAUGHTER

Summer evening, sunlight like a smile across our yard,
my daughter watches as I dip the bubble-wand
into the liquid-filled tube and, god-like, sweep my arm
across the air, filling the space around us with iridescent globes
that slowly turn and drift above the lawn, the rainbow colors
shifting on their surfaces like swirling continents.
My daughter, bubbling with joy, chases after them,
turning this way and that to grasp and hold them,
but world after impossible world bursts at her touch.
No matter. It is enough to touch,
and for a good long while I join her in this game
as each sphere bursts and returns its air to the sea of air
we breathe. Then my daughter tires and turns to me
to be held, so we sit in a chair and watch
the sun's red globe burst against the trees
and splash its light across the clouds.
As the sky darkens into blues and grays,
she turns to face me and fall asleep. I am content
to hold her and watch the twilight turn to dusk,
and the dusk to night, as if a wand beyond our knowing
slowly spreads across the sky and fills the space around us
with worlds beyond anyone's grasp. But I grasp enough
to know that in my brief time left breathing
on this turning globe, I hold the center in my arms.
And so I rise and turn to enter the house
and carry her up the difficult stairs to her bedroom
and lay her to sleep on her bed beneath the rainbow
we painted on her wall, her yellow wall, in her sun-yellow room,
above the ground, in our two-story red brick house.

THE FISH

after Lao Tzu

This afternoon I am watching a fly fisherman catch nothing
as he casts from the hot riverbank, his lure snagging at times
in wrangles of weeds and dead roots. For a moment, he pushes
back his hat and watches a few clouds drift effortlessly
eastward in a slow tail wind, then again begins
to cast his line as if he were whipping the river.
Timing is everything in fishing—and patience—and a little skill.
He missed the feed-time of early morning when insects hatch
in half-light and fall to the water's surface,
defenseless against what rises from below.
The river has its own time, as does everything living within it.
He should find his own time, spare the rod,
lie lureless in the shade, and drift eastward with his own current.
Hunger will rise naturally as the day ages and cools.
He will know then when to feed.

The Case Against Daedalus

He was a brilliant man who knew that life
as labyrinth can seem to never end, yet when
imprisoned, he himself could not imagine
the city inside the still dark point

of solitude and so, with his son, took flight.
His son's mistake, he says, was not of kind,
but of degree, yet Daedalus must have known
the fuse of youth is lit by admonition,

that a couple of singed wings are nothing
compared to flying higher than dad. Besides,
his son was young, and the young are always immortal.
Daedalus must have known. We know he sought

to murder his gifted nephew, whose inventions
began to outshine his own. We know he wanted
to be the only sun of art and was willing
to melt any wings that approached his height.

But the centers of suns are darker than solitude
and full of heaviness. What else could feed such light?
Radiance is the art of darkness, not a matter of flight
towards or above, but of gravity within.

At a Construction Site with My Son

"How do they know what to build?" he asks
as we watch a man hammer a nail to join
two carefully measured boards as one.
"They have a plan that someone made," I say,
which seems to satisfy him as he smiles
with a gentleness as warm as springtime sun.
I think about the nature of plans, how
the man with the hammer clearly has intent,
which requires—what?—awareness? which
itself requires what? I come like some
incompetent explorer paddling upstream
to the same impassable falls of logic,
always stopping at the edge of the wilderness
that lies beyond our thought…

I think of the days of my son's construction,
the moment of conception, the brink of the unseen,
and reach the same impassable falls of understanding.
Egg meets seed and building starts, but what
awareness precedes that? Perhaps when
egg-as-lock and seed-as-key fuse,
The Door opens, the spirit-portal into flesh,
and Awareness enters, receives its body's
blueprint from the parents' bodies' blueprints
and builds its home in the mother's haven.
Perhaps.
            However it was and is, he's come
a long way to be here today, a universe
of his own, swirling with galaxies of cells
that hold his shape and allow that-which-he-is
to gather the tissues of his face into this
precise expression of love I call *his smile*.

A GENETICALLY ENGINEERED SUPERHUMAN LAMENTS

I'm not saying I want to degenerate
to the times when malformed bodies imprisoned

our minds, and lives were lost to bio-bits,
and billions fumbled in fogs of ignorance

with a common intellect as close to ours as pets,
but we've pruned the tree of human genealogy

to a few straight branches. We're spires aspiring
to ourselves. We're stars crowding in a darkness

of too much light, and nobody wants to constellate.
Lately, after another perfect night

of gods and goddesses, I've lain awake, wondering
what I might have been had my parents' genes

formed an unplanned peace between them,
meeting deep in the dark forest of my mother's

body like two lovers, alone, confessing
their imperfections in the private honesty of love.

THE IMAGE

To save his father, Aeneas carried Anchises
out of the flames of Troy on his shoulders,
leaving the robes and golden bowls to the Greeks,
who tore and rummaged through the bleating city.

He carried him to the hollow valley past
the funeral mound and ancient cypress, only
to find he had to risk his life again
to save his wife who had not followed in the rush.

He haunted the streets until her ghost appeared
and told him to leave with only her absence,
and so Aeneas, deep inside the night,
returned to Anchises and sat beneath the wounded

moon and sharp stars until his father spoke,
dropping a few globed words like stones
into the pool of silence, the rings of significance
widening all the way to their lives' edge…

Speak carefully now. The future is busy
and will carry on its back from the flames
only what it cannot bear to lose.

The Bridge

A bird's song echoes through the quiet woods
where a stone bridge arcs from bank to bank
across a mirroring stream fringed with trees.
Its gray stones are so precisely joined
that the arch and its reflection on the water
form a perfect circle like a mouth or eye
opened in quiet wonder or surprise.

Though I know that I in time must cross it,
I am in no hurry. I wonder how long
this ancient stream's been flowing between the echoing
stone and the earth, into the dark portal
and its unquenchable thirst. I have only
a little time before I have to leave,
but time enough for an eye to open fully
to the stream of experience, and a mind to carefully
fashion something to arc from here to there,
shaping what I know, to reflect and complete
itself on the flow of what I don't.

WORDS FOR MY WIFE

As we lie on the riverbank of our life,
your head pillowed on my arm as you sleep,
I am taken again by the shining
black rivergrass of your hair, by the fringed
crescents of your closed lids in the morning light,
by your warm body, fresh in bed, a choir of smiles,
fragrant as bread. Soon you will awaken, wipe
the sleepcrust from your eyes, and smile at me,
the gleam of dreaming still clinging like a sheet
of water to your emerged skin, and one more time
in the long stream of our love, we may braid
and unbraid through an entire day of stones
or else commingle in a long slow pool
of affection. There are no perfect lives,
we know that, but we've had times filled with peace
like summer evenings bathed in amber light.
Tonight, we may again have such a time, or we may not.
But know this: after my clouded body rains
to the earth, you may sit with me at any time without sadness,
the arms of memory enfolding you with the preserved goodness
of these years, our light abiding through whatever dark
places you must pass, until Time, which forgets
none of us, remembers to carry you, finally, back to me.

What Saves Us

I.

It's the little things that pierce, sometimes,
the points of pain, numerous as gnats,
that we label sentimental so we can turn
our backs to live. Each one could claim us
entirely, if we let it, until a sea
of tiny hands would pull us down to grief.

And so, the kitten crushed in rushing traffic
as it crossed towards its mother must not matter
more than we can bear, more than one
more flake in the drifts of darkness, more
than one more cell in the body of despair.

Besides, we were helpless to help, and all
had somewhere to cross to, some other side,
here, in this wincingly beautiful world
where innocence is the briefest flower on earth.

II.

It's the little things that save us, sometimes,
in the season of aftermath, after birds
have filled the autumn skies like dark notes
in the music of departure, after they have streamed
away in long tapers of grief, and pain's
unspeakable magnitudes have left us mute
as mown fields filled with snow, mute
as the snow itself falling like ash through leafless
branches, like sand through outstretched hands.

The list of bitter things is now a ponderous book
that none of us can lift. But the little things
can save us, sometimes, in our grief.

There's a tenderness inside us that persists
at cross-purposes to our driven days
and scar-thickened skins. It reaches through
our barricades to gather the grains of kindness
and of joy we find scattered through our lives,
the grains of light by which a darkened world can live.

The Andiron

"summon a vision and declare it pure…"
                    from "In a Dark Time" by Theodore Roethke

The night is cold and clear, the windows edged with frost.
A full moon casts a milk-white sheen on everything.
Trees stand gleaming in our yard as tall as shepherds
above the flocks of shrubs. We warm before our fireplace
as four logs burn in the andiron's arms.
It's late, and I'm the only one awake, the others
lulled to sleep by the murmuring flames and the muffled sounds
of the outside traffic settling down, its sirens and horns
less frequent now. Our fire's flickerings cast an orange
glow on the eggshell walls we nest inside,
as I hold our toddler daughter on my chest beside
my wife, who holds our nursing son against her breast.
My daughter's breathing seems to synchronize with mine
like two bellows feeding our flame in perfect time.
With the quiet and quilting warmth, I'd stay forever if
I could, but the logs are ticking like clocks as they age
into ash and heat. The bottom two already are starting
to sift beneath the grate. I am not afraid to spend
what life I have each day providing warmth and light. Besides,
who knows how far beyond our days our lives might reach?
Even in death, it seems, these logs—once trees—have life:
all heat and light, their flame-leaves rise in the unseen
air like spirit-trees branching to another sphere.
On nights like this I hear, beneath the midnight whisperings
of the house, the dark bellows of the universe breathing
in and out, and think: *Everything is held.*
Unseen eternal flames spread green warmth through the world.
Then, when I rise to carry my child upstairs to sleep,
I hear a siren screaming from a distant street.

STAGE IV

There are no sidewalks in our neighborhood,
just lawns that reach to gutters along our streets
where each morning we would see him shuffle by,
his bone-slats body draped in shirt and slacks,
and his face as taut as lampshade skin.
He strained to move as though he dragged
a sack of rocks behind him.
In the heart's core, the small white pilot
light of life must not give up, and so
each day he rose by force of will
to live, against the downward pull
of measured poisons heavy in his blood,
and purpled radiation burns along his neck,
and the long fresh wounds the surgeon left.

At night the earthworms in our lawns emerge
to crawl in the open air, free from struggling
through the soil, and safe from the flaring sun.
Some venture from the dew-moist grass
to crawl along our streets, but blind,
they only feel their way and fail to reach
the lawns again by dawn. Each day
he'd find them dragging at his feet, lost
and covered in dust, and soon to die on streets
that get as hot as griddles in the summer heat.
Weak as he was, we'd see him stoop
to find a little twig or stem-end of a fallen leaf,
and use it like a staff to lift the little beings
to the green pastures where they belonged and longed to be.
We'd see this every day. Every day we'd see
his little acts of kindness, his earnest wordless prayer.

Theology Pondered in a Night Café

God—
the word itself is like a fog at sea.
The Truth is hard to see.
With telescopes and microscopes, we search
the platelets of galaxies to the brink of time
and galaxies of cells to the seam of matter
itself. What *is* It, through our eyes,
that is seeking to Divine Itself in the dark?

And what Omnipotence would want to glove Itself
in matter, especially the infant gloves of innocence
that are torn and ripped in the work of this world?

Does the heavy weightlessness of Eternal Being
find relief in brief precipitations
into matter and individual form?
Like a sleepless playwright, deep in the Night Café,
does It fracture Itself into characters to create a play?

Does Eternal Wakefulness sometimes also need to sleep
and dream our dreams of loneliness and incompleteness,
to dream our whole eternally perishing cast of dreams?

What if once—like now, for instance—a minor
character would speak out of turn and whisper
with a tiny voice in the Playwright's mind, "wake up!"
would we all just vanish?

Late Autumn

A butterfly searches our garden plants for blossoms
 I don't see. Flitting, almost lurching, it lands
   at last on a barren branch as if exhausted
     and now sits perfectly still. Nectar days

are clearly at an end, yet it looks

     like a blossom itself, like a little Buddha
    in the year's last light. Perhaps it finds
   the flower of consciousness, when wing-petals
awaken and lift above our stems in buttered flight.

SPHERES

My wife is heavy with new life and rests
in her reclining chair, fully sphered
and shining. Our son is almost born and pushes
against the boundaries of his space as his little
hands and feet make tiny bulges on
the mother's globe that quickly come and go.
He's learning language in the womb, we're told,
so I lean close to the mother-world, where he
lies curled inside, and speak to him, down
through the layers of nesting globes (or up, if it's true
that we have fallen from childhood). At first I worry
that he doesn't hear his ghostly father
in the dim darkness of the thrumming sea
and pulsing rush of aortal surf, but then
wherever I speak he reaches to *that spot*
as if trying to touch my voice, here, on the other
side. I think how soon his life in the mother-sea
will end, and how he'll be born into this sea
of air where we'll be waiting for him, and how
the sea-pulse will suddenly grow distant
and haunt his future years along the shore.
I think of those who all their lives have heard
a voice calling from the other side,
how they answer in prayers from the edge of our world
and sometimes raise their hands to the enveloping sky,
pleading or praising, and sometimes even in their last
moments tremble not with fear, but joy
at soon being born into what we call "death."
I think of our kind, bearing ourselves through nesting
spheres of land and sea, then air, then space,
seeking the face of truth. I wait. I listen.

Meditation Caves of Tibet

The land has risen many times into mountains
only to be clawed back down again
by the mindless trinity of wind, ice, and rain.
In Tibet, the Himalaya rises closer
to the upper edge of air than any other place
on earth, and yet it is falling even as it lifts.
The sheer cliffs of the Upper Mustang are crumbling
into streams, and its hillsides rut like ancient skin.
There was a time when even this highest kingdom,
this abode of the snow, was only a seafloor,
a batter of stones, sand, mud, shells,
and all the other fallen things that had sifted
downward through an ancient sea to make its bed,
but in time it all was pressed into rock and lifted
skyward.

No wonder Buddhist monks who turned
two thousand years ago from the churn of the turning
world rose among these barren rocks
and thin air to find their secret space.
Hundreds of feet from the ground in a cliff's face,
they carved their doorways into the rock, square
and half-wheel portals you can see from below.
They knew their bodies were just a brief dream
of the earth, a little dust and water risen
together somehow, for a time. So they entered
the heart of the rock to watch the rise and fall
of their own breath and to let all thought
sift from the clarity of their being, gazing
sometimes at an image they painted on the blank page
of their inner wall, and speaking at times the same
words over and over into the unseen air,
their faint sounds rising, possibly, to the surface
of our atmosphere and opening at last like rings
on a lake to a clarity beyond all matter,
imperceptibly to us, perhaps,
but audible enough for a spirit world to hear.

CPSIA information can be obtained
at www.ICGtesting.com
Printed in the USA
JSHW030926230420
5244JS00003B/9